WAITING ROOM LIMERICKS

or

YOU COULD DIE LAUGHING

WAITING ROOM LIMERICKS

or

YOU COULD DIE LAUGHING

by

Edwin J. Weinstein M.D., Ph.D.

Illustrated by David Baxter

Rhapsody Publications

Portland, Oregon

ISBN 0-9629424-7-2

Rhapsody Publishing Co. 7417 S.W. Beaverton-Hillsdale Hwy. # 510, Portland, OR 97225

This book is dedicated to all patients who may spend endless hours reading boring magazines in doctor's waiting rooms and who may then suffer the indignities of physical exams, be jabbed and poked while in the laboratory for specimens of blood and urine and then end up with a prescription which they can neither read nor understand. Or, they might later find themselves down the end of a scary hospital labyrinth in a mechanized bed or under the glare of operating lights and wonder how they got there.

It is also dedicated to the many doctors and other medical personnel who don't mind having fun poked at themselves.

Acknowledgements

I am deeply indebted to my daughter, Ruthanne, for editing the text, and to my daughter-in-law, Doe Risko who spent countless ours advising me on the intricacies of self publishing. Doe not only placed the limericks into a logical sequence, but was instrumental in the preparation of the page layouts. Without their help this book could not have been published.

I am also indebted to Grace, my wife, whose chuckling over the limericks encouraged me to keep going.

Foreword

These limericks were written for the fun of writing. They were written in off moments, when I drove back and forth to the clinic or the hospital, or at three o'clock in the morning when I couldn't sleep. They were meant to put a little humor into the sometimes grim life of modern medicine and to poke some fun at doctors and the medical establishment.

All of us, and that includes myself, have stories to tell about the horrors of long waits in barren waiting rooms, or misdiagnoses or of not understanding the doctor after he gives a lofty explanation. These limericks tell some of those stories but hopefully in a humorous form, and perhaps if they are read in a waiting room will make that wait a little more bearable. If they bring on a smile or a laugh, so much the better for all of us know 'laughter is the best medicine.

TABLE OF CONTENTS

HOSPITALIZATION

MEDICATION

BILLING THE PATIENT

THE DOCTOR'S WIFE, HIS NAME AND HIS NIGHTMARE

Next...

THE WAITING ROOM
AND DOCTOR'S OFFICE

COMMON MYTHS
THAT NEED REEVALUATION

It is said that an apple a day
Will help keep the doctor away.
   But if that apple were green
   With a worm in between,
You might wish for another entree.

A man with a devilish cold
By the great Linus Pauling was told
   To take vitamin C
   And from his cold he'd be free,
But he felt he'd been way oversold.

When nine out of ten use brand A
To keep a headache away.
   Why does the other
   Prefer still another,
Or wasn't he offered the pay?

Johnson who simply forgot
One day while exceedingly hot
    As he lay on his bed
    With a cloth to his head
Should he feed a fever or not?

But his wife who should have known better
Got a cold from some God-awful weather.
    Her best intuition
    Said fever needed nutrition
Or was it the reverse, altogether?

JUST WHERE IS THE DOCTOR'S OFFICE?

There once was a doctor named Clancy
Who lived on lower Delancy
　　Though the office seemed spare
　　He gave very good care
Though the treatment he gave wasn't fancy.

WHAT GOES ON IN THE WAITING ROOM?

The patients were lined up in rows
Depressed with all of their woes.
   Yet their doctor it seems
   Teed off in the greens
Why they stayed? Nobody knows.

What is a poor girl to do
When she comes for her appointment at two?
  Then is barely alive
  When she's examined at five
And told that, "It's only the flu."

While awaiting your turn to be seen
You're engrossed in an old magazine
 When the nurse calls your name
 You look up with disdain
Thinking thoughts that are almost obscene.

While waiting her turn to be seen
She re-read her third magazine.
 And from what she had learned
 She discovered what turned
Her urine to bright Kelly green.

WHO WERE SOME
OF THE MORE INTERESTING PATIENTS?

There was a young man of good note
Who bleated at times like a goat.
  Though it sounded bizarre
  They found a cigar - - -
The damn thing was stuck in his throat.

$2^{x^3}/y^3 \div$
$nc \sim \pi$
$\perp x^2/y_2$

There once was a teacher of math
With one leg short an inch and a half.
  He was consistently late
  For he couldn't walk straight
Since he required a circular path.

THE OCCASIONAL OUT OF TOWN PATIENT

There was a young vet from Tibet
And over each zit he would fret.
    Every promise for cure
    With ads of allure
Kept him for sure in great debt.

A man with no vent for his bile
Came drifting down on the Nile.
    He'd come for the cure
    To make his skin pure
And eliminate his verdigris smile.

Der wuz 'a niceman' from New Yawk
Whose tongue wuz da shape of a fawk.
  A doctah named Young
  Remodeled his tongue
To puts da ahs back when he'd tawk.

Dis man still couldn't say "ah"
Cause his tongue wuz now in a jah.
  He wuz decidedly woise
  Cause he made da wrong cherse
When his soijery toined out bizzah.

There once was a bald fellow named Ben
With a lump on his head, called a wen.
   But from its shape and its size
   You tried not to surmise
That it wasn't laid there by a hen.

There was once a funny masked stranger
Who looked like a man called 'lone ranger'.
   He'd been sitting of course
   Too long on his horse,
And his bottom was signaling 'danger'.

SOMETIMES
THE WRONG PATIENT GETS EXAMINED

There was once a fellow who drank
And whose mind would often go blank.
    When the nurse called, "George" or "Bill"
    He'd answer her, still,
His name was neither t'was Frank.

THE DOCTOR'S EXAM

This is what the doctor does best.
He waits 'til you're partly undressed.
    And with a hand that's like ice
    He doesn't think twice
As he places it onto your chest.

When doc said please open wide
So he could look down deeper inside
    Then didn't say naught
    Though he appeared deep in thought
It was the bad news his demeanor implied.

A spastic fellow named Kirk
Had reflexes that were more than berserk.
    When doc struck his patella
    This muscular fella
Kicked him a mile with his jerk.

Then they wrapped the blood pressure cuff
And squeezed the bulb with a puff.
    His nerves went on fire
    When his pressure rose higher,
He smiled, but it's all a big bluff.

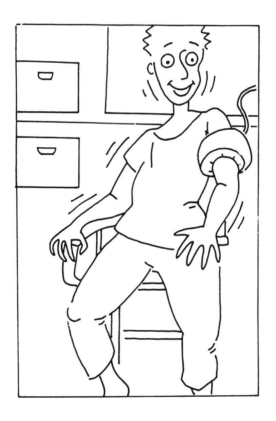

X - RAY

Poor Jim at the doctor's request
Had an X-ray exam of his chest.
   A spot that they found
   Was two inches round
'Twas a coin that showed through from his vest.

There once was a drummer called Sam
Who went in for a doctor's exam.
   He thought it quite neat
   To have the wild beat
That jazzed up his cardiogram.

Poor Jeff, saw his doc, said, "he's tired."
A vitamin was all he desired.
　　But the doc said he'd try
　　To find out just why
As a sloth, Jeff seemed to be mired.

He was examined from his head to his toe
To seek out the cause of his woe.
　　To be honestly frank
　　The doc came up with a blank
Told Jeff, to the lab he must go.

Jeff took each test in the book.
There were none he dared overlook.
　　From a forearm vein
　　He saw his blood drain
And the funds from his own pocketbook.

Stumbling and now unable to walk
Jeff then returned to his doc.
    "Tell me what's wrong
    This has gone much too long
And my home, I've now had to hock."

Said the doc, "I'm not being unkind
But it seems it was all in your mind.
    It would be better instead
    If we examined your head
And to a shrink, you'd start to unwind."

Poor Jeff in a desperate state
Went to a pub his tale to relate.
    The iron in wine
    Made him feel fine
And his thoughts he could now liquid-ate.

THE LABORATORY

WHAT ABOUT
THOSE MESSY LABORATORY TESTS?

The nurse said "I thank you a lot."
After the fellow had peed in the pot.
   "But, it isn't enough - - -
   I need more of this stuff."
"But it's all," he said, "that I've got."

AND THE WOMEN?

For men, the cups are easy to fill
They don't need a particular skill.
    But the girls filling up
    The specimen cup
May leave spots on the floor from a spill.

GENERAL MEDICAL PROBLEMS

TOBACCO AND DEMON RUM

A man to whom warnings were sung
Of the horrors of cigarette lung
    Coughed all in vain
    Till he ruptured his brain
With a fag 'tween his lip and his tongue.

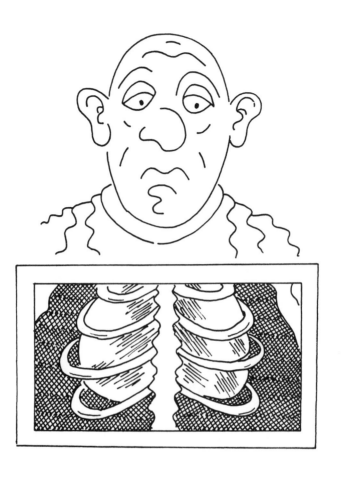

At the end of each bronchial tree
Are some sacs called alveoli
    And it isn't a joke
    When they're filled up with smoke.
No sir! 'tis just misery.

There was a young squirt from Pine Bluff
Who was admonished never to puff.
   Said he, "I'm no fool
   I'll follow the rule."
Then proceeded to sniff away snuff.

There was once a man from Flagstaff
Who drank wine from a carafe and a half.
   When advised to reduce
   The bubbly juice
He'd wink his eye and just laugh.

This man who very morose is
Because of his strong halitosis
    Would get rid of his stink
    If he'd give up his drink
It would also improve his cirrhosis.

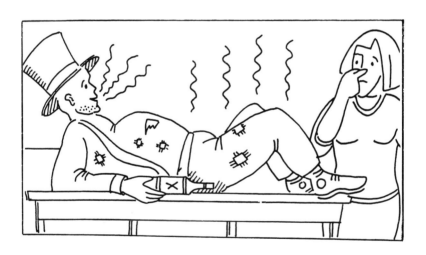

There once was a golden Apollo
Whose leg was thought to be hollow.
  Though he said with a wink,
  "I can down any drink."
It was more than most others could swallow.

There once was a souser whose sin
Was the over-consumption of gin.
  He said he would stop
  And switch to some pop.
I'm afraid his sin did him in!

THOSE PATIENTS

WITH WEIGHTY PROBLEMS

There once was a man in whose dream
He gobbled up mountains of cream.
    Then dreamt he died fat
    Though his name was Jack Sprat,
And was the skinny half of the team.

An overweight fellow named Bruce
Went through torture in attempts to reduce.
  A battle was raged
  Yet ten years he aged
Before he called it a truce.

Charles, a huge man from Mobile.
His weight he tried hard to conceal.
And he hoped it would seem
That the butter and cream
In his arteries wouldn't congeal.

Now this man who still answers to Charlie
Changed his diet to consist of plain barley.
But we'll never know why
He swallows it dry
Though it bloats him up by the yardley.

Here's my advice to persons obese
Who cannot their weight seem to decrease.
   "When you keep on a tryin'
   To avoid chicken that's fryin'
Just remember, it's odiferous grease."

And you're stumped on which diet to eat
As you're chomping away on your meat
   Then a burger and fries
   Are not the best buys
In reducing the size of your seat.

   Since folks eat more chicken or fish
   To comply with doctor's strong wish.
      But now if you please
      Since there's less heart disease
   The doc will no longer get rich.

There was a young fellow named Jake
Who choked on a huge piece of steak.
   It tasted so good
   He ate more than he should,
So now we're attending his wake.

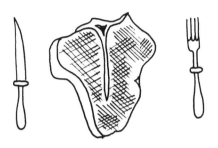

With cholesterol now on the run
Eating steak is no longer much fun.
   There's little sex appeal
   In a vegetarian meal
Even if served on a hamburger bun.

There was once a model called Lynn
Who yearned to be exceedingly thin.
    Diet pills that she took
    Gave her a new look
Now her widest part is her grin.

MENTAL PROBLEMS

A lass who once said in jest
That she was by the devil possessed.
   And thought she's a freak
   And somewhat unique
'til she learned she's just like the rest.

A fellow with a twin ego state
Was unable to others relate.
   But he saved his phone dime
   And oodles of time
Jawing with his alternative mate.

Dan was a manic depressive
Whose mood swings were wildly excessive.
    After a moment of calm
    He'd explode like a bomb
And display the side that's aggressive.

    Dan dosed on pills best not renamed.
    "He's cured!" the doctor exclaimed.
        But now he's so docile
        He looks like a fossil.
    His aggressive side has been tamed.

ASTHMA

A dismal young man who would sneeze
So hard he'd fall on his knees.
   He knew what was wrong
   He just didn't belong
Near pollen that came from the trees.

ARTHRITIS

Once said the doc, just to spite us,
Claimed Lee hadn't bursitis.
What he said in one breath
Just scared her to death.
He told her 'twas costochondritis.

Slim developed a pain in his back
And when treated you'd hear his bones crack.
Though twisted and bent
This astonishing gent
Enjoyed the Rx of a quack.

This man with his agonal pain
Whose joint would flare up in the rain
 Was even more pissed
 If there was only a mist.
A thing he found hard to explain.

There was once a fellow from Kent
Whose finger was awkwardly bent.
 His disfigured joint
 Would alter his point
And not in the direction he meant

PROBLEMS WITH VISION

There once were two men of a kind
Each in one eye was quite blind.
    Said one with a grin,
    "That's my identical twin,
And whatever I lose he will find."

When retrieved from the auto collision
Don said with the utmost derision,
"I wouldn't have swerved
If the road hadn't curved."
Though the cause was monocular vision.

There once was a women called Fay
Who chomped down six carrots a day.
   She believed the remark
   That she'd "see in the dark"
Though she was blind as a bat in the day.

GASTROINTESTINAL PROBLEMS

John who was flushed with elation
Had cause for a huge celebration.
When he found it was fruit
That could help him toot toot
And rid him of his constipation.

There was a young lad from Scappoose
Whose stools were incredibly loose.
    After many a try
    This frustrated guy
A firm version he did finally produce.

If you've eaten some food that's too ritz
And suddenly it feels like the pits.
    And you just have to go
    Don't tarry to slow
When you're having a run of the $f£º*@\^s$!

There once was a fellow named Murray
Whose vision often turned blurry.
    With eyes filled with tears
    And steam from his ears
He'd vowed he'd stop eating hot curry.

There once was a fellow called Gus
Whose burp caused a hell of a fuss.
    After spices he ate
    Let gas dissipate
As it rose up the esophagus.

There was once a man with a bowel
Which would rumble and emit a loud growl.
   Though as much as he tried
   His symptoms to hide
His neighbors would twitter and howl.

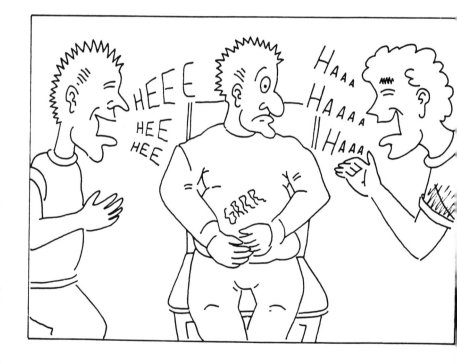

There once was a fellow called Rollo
Who agreed to a barium swallow.
   The thing that doc found
   Was that his gut was quite round
Not only that, he learned it was hollow.

There was once a fastidious nut
Who had a pacemaker installed in his gut.
   Now for his amusement
   He can dial his own movement
His irregularity is now anything but.

RESPIRATORY PROBLEMS

In and Ex were the Hales
Who were in charge of a noise called the rales.
    But do not despair
    That they lived simply on air
And their sighs were only contrails.

When Al eyed his yacht on the wharf
He developed a ticklish cough.
   I'll bet you a nickel
   That the throat with its' tickle
Developed to get the day off.

But the throat was worse than he thought
Cause it was a strep that he caught.
   When the throat turned bright red
   He headed for bed
And his plans they all came to naught.

There was once a man who too often
Had terrible spells of bad coughin.
   But it wasn't the cough
   That carried him off
It was the coffin they carried him off in!

After she came for a nasal inspection
She was told it was a complex infection.
   "It's half strep and half staph."
   She was told with a laugh,
How's that for a mixed up collection?

NO ONE IS HAPPY WITH ONE'S HEIGHT

When a tall man who found his great height
Put him on level of birds in their flight.
    When they asked why
    He had his head in the sky
He described the cause of his plight.

When he was young he developed the knack
Of getting a crick in the back.
    Despite the advice
    To use heat, and or ice
Instead he stretched out on the rack.

There once was a man much too short.
To his friends he gave this retort.
    Said he to his cronies,
    "I won't ride on small ponies,
For riding a horse is my sport."

INSOMNIA

Ralph was in trouble knee deep
For he often talked in his sleep.
  The things that he said
  Would turn faces red
And required a two-minute bleep.

And then there was Helen McKnight
Who woke up at two every night.
    When her alarm would chime
    At her getting up time
She'd be dead to the world, just for spite.

Her husband was the opposite way.
He'd nod off when his head hit the hay.
    From two until four
    He snort and he'd snore
Adding to Helen's dismay.

AGING

As smoke curled from the end of his pipe
Methuselah discoursed his lone gripe.
    Though at nine hundred and one
    The son of a gun
Said his wrinkles made him look overly ripe.

There once was a lady I know
Whose gait was exceeding slow.
  Though try as she might
  To keep up, her delight
Was to amble around on tip toe.

DERMATOLOGY

There once was a colorful fellow
Whose skin looked like lemony jello.
    It was the carrots he ate
    By the pound and the crate
That turned him from white into yellow.

There once was a man on the range
Who complained he was covered with mange.
    "What do you think?"
    He said to the shrink.
"I think your mind is quite strange!"

PATIENTS WHO JUST DO NOT UNDERSTAND

A maid with a simple complaint
Was told by the doc what it ain't.
    "But what have I got?
    I know what it's not.
I can't understand your explaint."

There was once a patient named Herman
Who told all his symptoms in German.
    Though the doctor spoke Spanish
    The symptoms would vanish
Though the language he knew not a word in.

THE DOCTOR GIVES ADVICE

There was a young man from Dubuque
Whose liver was the cause of rebuke.
   Said the doc to him, "Son,
   I know it's not fun
But that's why each morning you puke."

If you've got a "pressure condition"
Brought on they say, "by nutrition,"
   Then claim it's your fault
   Cause you eat too much salt
And will lead you straight to perdition.

And then I'd just like to mention
When on pills for fluid retention.
   A banana a day
   Keeps one's weakness away.
It's almost a standard convention.

The chap with a varicose vein
Who walked with the aid of a cane
    Was told it is said
    He should stand on his head
And let the silly thing drain.

There once was a lady from Corning
Whose symptoms returned without warning.
    Told "It wasn't too bad,
    So get back in the pad,
And be sure to call in the morning."

It's not true that the doc always knows best
When he listens to the noise in your chest.
    Says "Take in a deep breath"
    And you can hold it til death
He forgets that exhaling is next.

There once was a fine chappy named Buck
Who had a colt in Detroit and Kentuck.
    After doc looked in his throat
    He penned in a note.
On lemon drops he should suck.

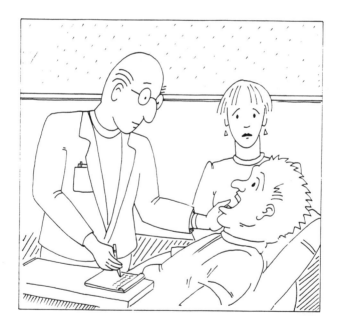

There once was a doctor who said
The tiredness is all in your head.
　　So get out the door
　　And exercise more - - -
And perk up your life instead.

So this guy with his head in the dump
Got him some iron to pump.
　　Took the doctor's advice
　　And exercised twice
To try to get out of his slump.

After trying to lift weights once more
There was a muscle in his back that he tore.
    With a bellowing tone
    He found himself prone,
And unable to get off the floor.

So this wretched miserable gent
Back by ambulance to the doctor he went.
    Now told what was best
    Was to "get lots of rest
And pour on the liniment."

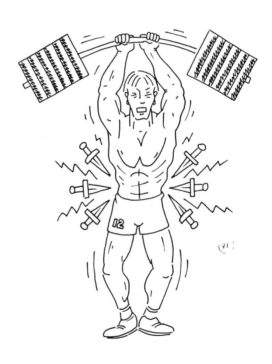

You could hear the violins fiddle
While you pondered this puzzling riddle.
    And you'd have to think twice
    About the diet advice
From the doc with a paunch in his middle.

When it's down with a cold you've been stricken
And you want the healing to quicken.
   Take this advice
   Take an aspirin twice
And to your soup add a boiled chicken.

PHYSIOLOGY

There once was a blood cell named White
Who loved to put up a good fight.
    He just put to ruin
    A bacterial goon
And their friends? He put them to flight.

White's cousin was Marvin the Red
He was a messy fellow who bled.
    He had nothing to do
    But to carry O_2
From the lungs to the arterial bed.

Sir Kidney had a foul tasting grin
As he parceled out drops of urine.
These were poured into tubes
That drained towards the pubes
And housed in a bladder therein.

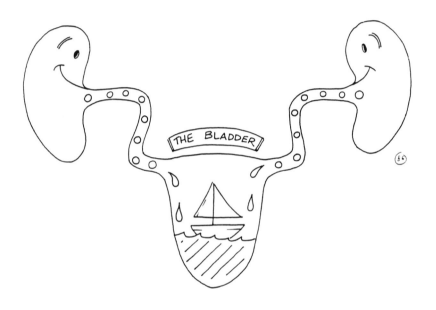

A general in the Army called Hugh
Was a patriot all the way through.
But 'tis sad to relate
His blood he couldn't donate
For the cells were red and white and blue.

PATIENTS QUESTION
THE DOCTOR'S SAGE ADVICE

There once was a patient called Bill
Who was given a tri-colored pill
   "Take doc's advice
   Swallow two of them twice
Or you'll soon be over the hill."

Said Bill, to the doc, "I'm inclined
To think that you're smart, but I find
   That those pills are so big
   They'd choke a stuffed pig
And the colors will soon make me blind."

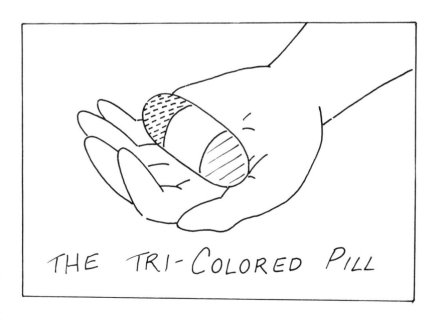

THE TRI-COLORED PILL

So Bill took the pills with a gripe
After hearing the doc's medical hype.
　　He did as he was told
　　And got rid of his cold,
But his skin had a three-colored stripe.

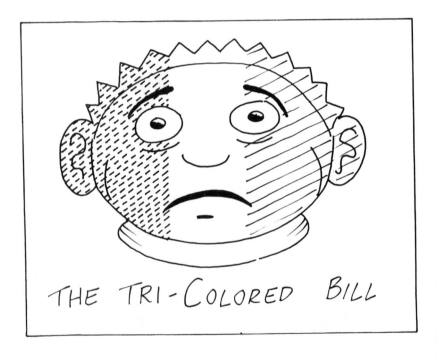

THE TRI-COLORED BILL

Jane came with a list that was long.
Told the doc he was treating her wrong.
   The doc shook his head
   And figured instead
The placebo he gave was too strong.

There was once a fellow named Ray
Who said in utter dismay,
"I really don't follow - - -
How can anyone swallow
The same pill three times a day?"

There once was a girl with a pain
Whose cause was sought, but in vain.
When she spent all her money
For tests, they said to her "Honey,
It must be because you're insane."

HOSPITALIZATION

ADMISSION

"I've got this terrible pain in my head."
"Fill out the form", the nurse said.
   "But by the time I get through
   With page one-hundred and two
Both you and I will be dead!"

IN THE HOSPITAL

The nurses in the hospital hall
Are clearly ignoring your call.
   Though they hear you quite well
   When you tinkle your bell
They seem to be having a ball.

There was a young girl in her bed
Who said, "It's not illness I dread
   But those terrible meals
   They roll in on the wheels
Which give me a pain in the head."

When you're filled with panic and gloom
The doc will burst into the room.
    He'll tell you you're fine
    Then spin on a dime,
And out of the room he will zoom.

There was a young man who by chance
Into a nurse's eyes did glance.
     Before he was aware
     He floated on air
And was definitely in a deep trance.

When you take to the halls for a stride
You'll develop a niche in your pride.
     For it becomes quite clear
     There's a draft on your rear
On the part that the gown doesn't hide.

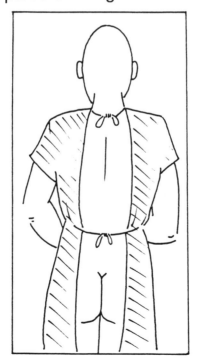

Said the nurse to the patient, "Oh dear,
Your symptoms are not very clear."
   With his attention diverted
   She quickly inserted
The thermometer into his rear.

There once was a man with a groan
Who produced such a melodious tone
    That folks far and near
    Would at his bedside appear
While he trumpeted his passage of stone.

The nurse said the food is quite good
So eat it she said, "If you would,
    Don't think of the taste
    Or feel its thick paste
Or you'll dream you ate some raw wood."

Carl had a treacherous slip
He skidded and busted one hip
    Doc said with a grin,
    "We can put a pin in
And soon you can do a backflip."

Side rails were raised on Carl's bed
For it is safer post-op, it is said.
    But when they were raised
    The doc was amazed
When Carl flipped onto his head.

So let me a little digress
For Carl, I confess, is a mess
    He's now chained to his bed
    To mend his sore head
And will be there for a while, I would guess.

Another rough dude from Pine Bluff
Who claimed he was wiry and tough.
But when given a shot
Believe it or not
He'd faint, like a cream puff.

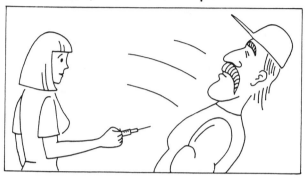

There was a bed-ridden woman named Fran
Whose strong urge was to get to the can.
The nurse said to her, "Dearie,"
In a voice that was cheerie,
"There's a ban on the can; use the pan."

SURGERY

There was once a man with six toes
Who lost a thumb when he froze.
    Said he to himself
    "With this God-given wealth
From my foot to my hand I'll transpose."

The surgeon was up to his knees
After cutting one of the V.P.s
    He was heard to say "oops"
    After one of his whoops
Mumbling- "There goes one of my fees."

There once was a surgeon I knew
Who practiced calligraphy too.
   In each new inscision
   He'd cut with precision
His own little curlicue.

There once was a surgeon of note
Who liked to read what he wrote.
   He thought he'd gain fame
   If he signed his full name
Into each little scar for a quote.

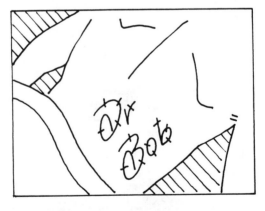

There once was a surgeon whose sight
Was a little bit less than all right.
　　When his patient awoke
　　It wasn't a joke
For his rear was sewed up a mite tight.

There once was a man who would bitch
About a spot on his back that would itch.
　　"I may be a crock
　　But I'll murder the doc
Who left in that ridiculous stitch."

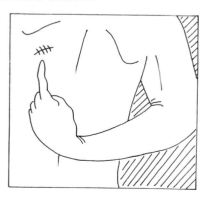

Doc waltzed in with a gown and a mask
Before starting his surgical task
  "But why am I here
  With my terrible fear
When I still have ten questions to ask?"

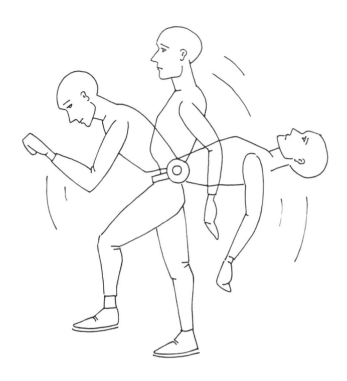

A man who could not bend to his toes
Told the surgeon the cause of his woes.
   After a surgical binge
   And a two jointed hinge
Now forward and backwards he goes.

PLASTIC SURGERY

There was a prize fighter called Lynn
Who was scarred for life on his chin.
Though the surgeon was plastic
His hand was quite spastic
Leaving Lynn with a one sided grin.

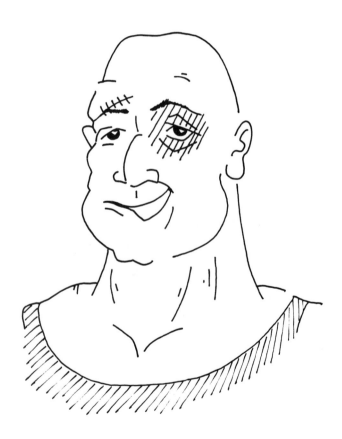

The woman gave her doc a request
To enlarge the size of her breast.
    With the increase in size
    She could capitalize
Figuratively on a life with more zest.

There was once a maid with a pimple
To have it removed was quite simple.
    It was cut out with a knife
    And for the rest of her life
In its place she was left with a dimple.

There once was a lady called Rose
Who was ashamed of the shape of her nose.
   So she had it arranged
   To have the shape changed
Only now it honks when she blows.

URINARY PROBLEMS

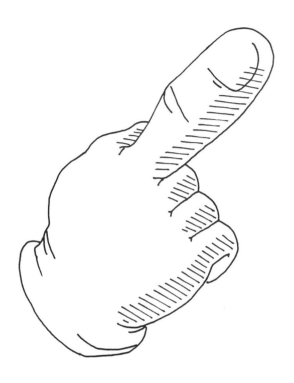

While face down in a bent over position
Said the gent to his stalwart physician,
    "I can't seem to figure
    How your finger gets bigger
When you examine my prostatic condition."

There was once a man we'll call Moe
Whose piddle was exceedingly slow.
   After his prostrate was drilled
   His wish was fulfilled
To write his name in the snow.

This man with a prostate disorder
Had difficulty passing his water
   'til his tube was reamed out
   And now out of the spout
It's coming out more like it oughter.

SEXUAL PROBLEMS

There was once a good looking sister
Who had a painfully prominent blister.
    Yet it wasn't so bad
    If only it had
Not occurred where he kissed her.

There was once a lady called Jill
Who was supposedly taking the pill.
    But one day she forgot
    And that's how she got
A bounder, ten pounder called Bill.

A young rake with a venereal curse
While getting a shot by the nurse
    Was told he'd better heed to
    His gung-ho libido
Or he'd be dragging his heels in a hearse.

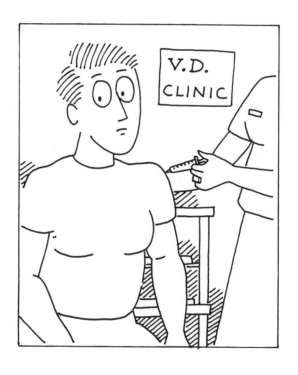

THE NEWBORN

There was once a babe in a womb
Who decided he needed more room.
　　"Gotta get out of this place
　　Cause I'm needing more space."
He said, as he entered the flume.

The newborn thought it ain't fair
To be held upside down in the air.
　　"What have I done
　　To get slapped on the bun
And get exposed to the chill of the air?"

While they were jammed in the birthing canal
Said the unborn twin to his pal
   "When the membrane is burst
   Why don't you go first
And make a break from the confines of this jail?"

DENTISTRY REFERRALS

Jim's jaws were clenched in contraction
But opened them only a fraction
    When the dentist said, "Wider!
    So I can put this inside yer,
And yank out the confounded impaction."

But this young man from Duluth
Was the victim of a monstrous goof.
  He was driven insane
  And had double the pain
When the dentist had pulled the wrong tooth.

ENDOCRINE PROBLEMS

There once was a fellow named Burt
Whose feelings were terribly hurt.
    If one very discreet is
    It won't help his diabetes
To remind him to stop eating dessert.

But Burt was a monstrous lout
Whose girth was exceedingly stout.
    He'd stay jammed in a chair
    And not walk on a dare
So he could nurse his foot with the gout.

FEVER

They nearly kissed Tommy good-bye
Cause his fever was reaching the sky.
    Though his goose was near cooked
    What they all overlooked,
Was his blanket, t'was turned up too high.

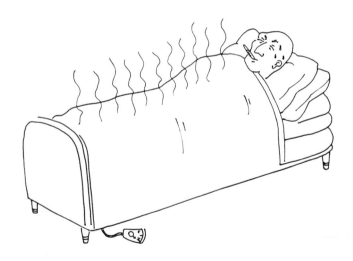

CARDIAC PROBLEMS

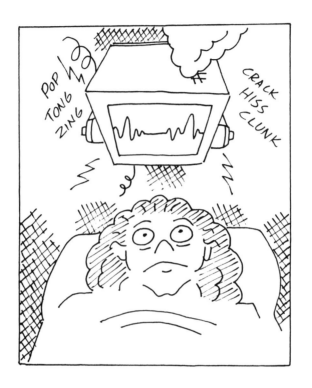

There once was a young city slicker
Whose pulse would occasionally flicker.
    He was one of those lugs
    Whose dependence on drugs
Caused a glitch in the niche of his ticker.

There once was a creature called Jack
Who had an angina attack.
    So a balloon was inserted
    And surgery averted
As well as a month in the sack.

MEDICATION

FROM THE PHARMACY

There was once a doctor whose writing
Could hardly be considered inviting.
　　He scribbled his words
　　Till they all looked absurd - - -
The results were less than exciting.

After a prescription or two were refilled
And the patient's symptoms were stilled
　　You couldn't be sure
　　If he got the cure
Or because the patient was killed.

There once were two brothers called Smith
One said to the other, "What if
    We could make a cough drop
    That could a cough stop?
We'd be rich," said he, "in a jif."

There once was a man who looked creepy
Cause the drugs he was on made him sleepy.
    So this lumbering buffoon
    Slept until past noon
Before emerging from his tri-colored teepee.

SOME STOPPED THE MEDICATIONS ON TIME

HOSPITAL

There was a gent for a while
Who seemed a bit dull and senile
    'Til he threw out the jug
    That held his new drug
And now can strut out in grand style.

SOME OVERDOSED ON MEDICATIONS

Francois was looped to the gills
After swallowing seventy pills
He said, "C'est la guerre."
When he took up the dare
To seek one of life's silly thrills.

But Francois was doubly blessed
For those pills he couldn't digest.
His thrill was usurped
When the pills he up-burped
And maybe you guessed the rest.

For those pills were not for elation
But were those that caused a sedation.
　　So his eyes he did close
　　Crossed his hands in repose
And hibernated for the duration.

SOME TRIED THEIR OWN REMEDIES

A young man who sat in the dew
Developed a horrible flu.
    He thought he'd feel better
    If his nose was less wetter
So he stopped up his nostrils with glue.

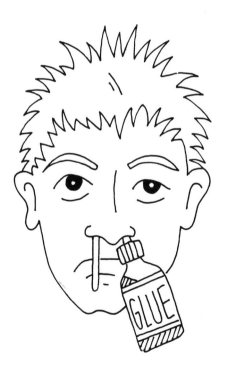

After Tom had his steroid injection
He thought he could avoid a detection.
   Though he ran a good race
   He was soon in disgrace
When his urine had failed the inspection.

BILLING THE PATIENT

DOCTOR'S FEES

There once was a doc who was willing
To assist in a merciful killing.
    Though it was all quite discreet
    He'd gotten cold feet
When it came to handle the billing.

Poor Will had a devilish plight
Said doc "Don't get so uptight."
    Said Will, "It's not funny
    I can't pay you the money."
Now guess who's not feeling quite right?

There once was a lass with a rash
Which circled her head like a sash.
    When she tried to erase
    The rash from her face
The doc told her he needed more cash.

The doc said his pain was a fake
Or simply "just a headache"
    So he gave him a pill
    The pain, for to kill
And presented the bill at his wake.

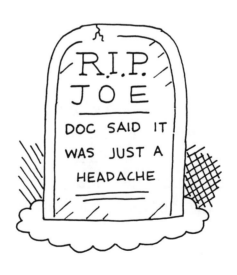

THE DOCTOR'S WIFE,
HIS NAME AND HIS NIGHTMARE

THE DOCTOR'S WIFE

If the doctor really knows best
And gives out great info with zest,
    Why do some doctor's wives
    Live miserable lives?
And the hours he puts in, they detest.

WHY A DOCTOR CHANGES HIS NAME

There once was a doctor of mine
Who went by the name of Weinstein,
    So after venting his spleen
    When they called him "Weinsteen"
He changed his name to O'Brian.

A DOCTOR'S NIGHTMARE

THE TABLES ARE TURNED

The doctor was deep in his gloom
In his dreams he could see a gray tomb.
    He dreamt he must wait
    Behind Peter's great gate
And be called last from the big waiting room.

GLOSSARY

Alveoli: Air cells at the end of the bronchial tree

Bile: Greenish yellow fluid secreted by the liver, stored in the gall bladder and may cause jaundice if not properly excreted.

Bursitis: inflammation of a bursa, or sac which lines a joint and if inflamed may cause pain.

C'est la guerre:That's war.

Cirrhosis: A disease of the liver, a common affliction of those that overindulge in alcoholic beverages

'Colt in Detroit and Kentuck': A cold in the throat and can't talk

Costochondritis: Inflammation of a rib and its cartilage, often painful

Diabetes: A disorder characterized by an increase in urine production. Diabetes mellitus, a disorder of carbohydrate metabolism

Fag: slang for cigarette

Flume: Birthing canal

Gout: an arthritic condition caused by deposits of uric acid in the joints. A common site is in a large toe joint

Halitosis: Offensive breath

Impaction: Condition of being firmly lodged or wedged

In and Ex were the Hales: Inhalation and Exhalation

Linus Pauling: Nobel Prize recipient, has done extensive investigation of medical benefits of Vitamin C

Mange: A skin disorder caused by mites affecting animals, occasionally humans

Marvin the red: A red cell

Methuselah: A patriarch who lived 969 years. Gen. 5:27

Monocular: Pertaining to or having one eye

New Yawk: New York City

Odoriferous: emitting an odor

Pan: bedpan

Patella: knee cap

Placebo: A substance having no pharmacological effect but given merely to satisfy a patient who supposes it to be a medicine.

Prostate: An organ that surrounds the urethra of males at the base of the bladder.

Pubes: The lower part of the abdomen

Puke: Slang, to vomit

Rales: Any abnormal respiratory sound heard in auscultation, and indicating some pathologic condition

Reamed out: A trans urethral resection of the prostrate, commonly called a TURP

Rx: Latin symbol for recipe

Trumpeted passage of stone: There is frequently extreme pain when calculi such as gouty concretions or calcium stones pass down the ureters

Tri Colored teepee: My version of an oxygen tent

Varicose: Abnormally or unusually enlarged or swollen

Venereal: Due to or propagated by sexual intercourse

Verdigris: A bluish green color

Wen: A sebaceous cyst especially on the scalp

Zit: A pimple or skin blemish

INDEX

About the Author

Edwin J. Weinstein M.D., Ph.D, born and raised in New York City, schooled in Chicago, moved west and spent over 25 years practicing internal medicine in Portland, Oregon. While seeing and treating thousands of patients, listening to their stories and their gripes and occasionally as a patient himself, he saw a different side of medical practice. That side, the humorous side is the side that he wants to share.

About the Illustrator

David L. Baxter, also of Portland, is branching out from his career as a graphic artist. The illustrations in this book displays his unique talents as a cartoonist.

Order Form

For Additional Copies of WAITING-ROOM LIMERICKS
(You could die laughing) send order form to:

Rhapsody Publications
7417 S.W. Beaverton-Hillsdale Hwy., Suite #510
Portland, Or 97225

Please send me _____ copies at $9.95 each   _____

Shipping:
Book Rate: $2.00 for first book and
75 cents for each additional.   _____

Payment:
__Check   __Money Order   Total enclosed   _____

Name: _____

Address: _____

City:_____State:_____Zip:_____- _____

Order Form

For Additional Copies of WAITING-ROOM LIMERICKS
(You could die laughing) send order form to:

Rhapsody Publications
7417 S.W. Beaverton-Hillsdale Hwy., Suite #510
Portland, Or 97225

Please send me _____ copies at $9.95 each   _____

Shipping:
Book Rate: $2.00 for first book and
75 cents for each additional.   _____

Payment:
__Check   __Money Order   Total enclosed   _____

Name: _____

Address: _____

City:_____State:_____Zip:_____- _____